MW01681369

Use The C -Word

A Simple Guide to Creating a Balanced Life

Paula B. Leed

eBook ISBN: 9798868902901

Paperback ISBN: 9798868902734

Published by Long Story Short Publishing Company

http://bestsellerservices.com

Printed in United States of America

Contents

Dedication

Every morning, my father would rise with a joyful proclamation: "Hello, world! Good morning, world!" Then he'd call out to me, urging me to greet the day with the same enthusiasm. I did then—and I still do. Each day, I feel grateful to wake up, greet the world, and refuse to let a few bad apples spoil the whole bushel. My mother shared that same radiant spirit. Her positivity was a constant light in our lives. Always and forever, I dedicate my life—and this book—to them both.

Thank you, Bernie and Sel, aka Mom and Dad. Your love lives in every word.

Having Courage is a daily decision.

1

The Courage to Begin

Courage is like that friend who's always there to push you out of your comfort zone even when you'd *rather* stay in bed with a cup of coffee and a cozy blanket! It's that little voice inside you that says 'you've got this' even when the world outside is telling you otherwise.

Courage isn't about the absence of fear; it's about taking ACTION – DESPITE the fear! It's about stepping forward even when your knees are shaking and your heart is racing. It's about having the confidence to face the unknown, knowing that every step you take is a step toward growth and self-discovery.

Let's dive into how courage plays a huge role in our lives from the small, everyday moments, to the big, life-changing decisions.

The Everyday Acts of Courage: The Unknown. aka: What's Behind the Curtain

Courage doesn't always have to be about our grand gestures or heroic deeds. In fact, sometimes courage emerges in small, everyday moments. It's the courage to speak up when you see something that's not right. It's the courage to try something new, even when you're not sure you'll succeed.

For example, think about the first time you tried a new hobby or stepped into a new job. There was that moment of hesitation, the flutter of doubt, the "Do I really want to do this" feeling... but you took that step anyway, didn't you?

That small act of courage often became a steppingstone to something wonderful! How often do we surprise ourselves with moments of quick decisions that change our lives forever in a Good Way! (okay, not always, but you won't know unless you try!)

Courage and Compassion

Courage is closely linked with compassion. It takes courage to be compassionate, to open your heart to others, to offer a listening ear for a helping hand. It is about being brave enough to show empathy. It's about having the gumption and understanding even when it's not the easiest thing to do.

Think about the times when you've seen someone struggle and felt that tug at your heart to help them. It takes courage to act on that compassion, to step forward and make a difference in someone's life, no matter how small it may seem. As I always say and repeat, these are some of the best and most rewarding moments in one's lifetime. Don't sell yourself short; when life hands you these special moments, accept them with grace and humility. They will often stand out in your mind as most memorable if not life-altering in your lifetime.

Courage and Confidence

While this may seem like a stretch, courage also intertwines with confidence. It's about truly believing in yourself, even when the odds seem stacked against you. It's about trusting that you have what it takes to overcome challenges and achieve your goals no matter how unrealistic they may seem.

Remember the first time you stood up for yourself, whether it was in a classroom, at work, or in a personal relationship? That moment of standing up, despite the fear of judgment or rejection, was an act of courage that built your confidence, even if you didn't realize it at the time.

Revolving your life around what I call the "C" words, we are going to create a path to continuous joy using my favorite 3: Courage, Compassion, and finally, and the MOST important, Common Sense! So, let's dive right in and see how your life will change for the better using and living by the "C" words!

Let's get started!

Our attitude toward life determines life's attitude toward us.

2

The Superpower Called Calmness

We've all been there. The To-Do List is never ending, the emails pile up like a mountain of paperwork, and the world feels like it's spinning a bit too fast. In times like these, it's easy to think that calmness is a luxury only those with endless vacation days or the ability to meditate for hours on end can enjoy. But the truth is, calmness isn't just for yogis on mountain tops. It's something you can grab, even in the busiest moments, and is more accessible than you might think.

Now, I know what you're probably thinking... Sure, calmness sounds nice, but I'm already juggling ten things at once! And I get it, life is not exactly designed to be stress free, but calmness doesn't mean avoiding life's challenges. It means learning how to approach them with a clear mind and a steady heart.

Let's take a step back for a second. Calmness is like this proverbial "calm at the center of a storm." While the winds of life whip around us with their demands, expectations, and never-ending to-do lists, calmness is the part of you that stays still. It's the ability to catch your breath, look around, and think clearly amid chaos. It's the pause that keeps you grounded.

But calmness isn't a magic switch you flip on or off (although wouldn't that be nice)? It's more like a muscle that you strengthen over time. And the best part? It is one of those most powerful tools in your toolbox that you can use to live a healthier, more positive life!

Calmness is more than just a fancy word. So why is it so important? Sure, it sounds nice to be calm but what does it do for you?

Calmness impacts your physical health, your mental well-being, and even your relationships. Practicing calmness daily is one thing that people do not talk about when they are navigating how to live a more stress free productive happy life. Sure, it sounds nice to be calm, but what does it actually DO for you? Well, let's break it down.

First off, calmness isn't about just sitting still and hoping the world slows down around you. It's about how you respond to life's curveballs.

Studies show that when we stay calm, we make smarter decisions, lower our stress levels, and even boost our immune systems. Sounds like a superpower, right? Well, why not look at it as one!

Imagine being stuck in traffic (the worst traffic you can imagine), you're already running late, and your blood pressure is skyrocketing through your imaginary sunroof. You could let stress take over, curse the world, and get even more anxious, or you could take a deep breath, listen to a calming podcast, and accept that right now, the best thing you can do is... well, stay calm!

The latter option isn't about Denying the frustration-it's about accepting that the situation is beyond your control, yet you still have the power to CONTROL your reaction. No one says you must LIKE the situation, but you certainly can approach it with calmness. And guess what? That's when you start feeling a sense of control again, which ironically helps you get through chaos more effectively!

But "how do we stay calm?" you ask.

Here's the kicker: Calmness isn't something you just *have* or *don't have.* It's a SKILL, one that we can cultivate with practice. Who Knew?!

It's not about magically becoming the Zen master of your universe, although I must say, That WOULD be FUN! It's about little, daily habits that train your mind and body to respond more calmly over time.

One great way to start practicing calmness is through mindfulness. Mindfulness doesn't require fancy equipment or seven hours of meditation. It's about paying attention to the present moment without judgment. So, next time you're in a meeting, stuck in traffic, or trying to make a tough decision, try pausing for just a moment. Take a few deep breaths, acknowledge your feelings, and allow yourself to settle into the moment. It's like a mini reset button for your brain.

And then, there's the power of perspective. A lot of times, the stress we feel reflects how we view a situation. We might think, this is a "disaster," when it's just an inconvenience. When you shift your perspective, you start realizing that not everything is a big deal. Life is full of bumps but most of them don't require you to lose your cool.

The Ripple Effect: How Calmness Effects Everything Around You

Here's a fun fact. When you stay calm, you not only improve your own well-being, but you also influence everyone around you. Ever notice how your stress levels seem to rise when the people around you are stressed? The same works in reverse. When you maintain a sense of calm, others are more likely to mirror that behavior.

This is especially true in relationships. When you're able to stay calm in challenging conversations or disagreements, you create space for healthy communication and resolution. The calmer you are, the more likely it is that others will stay calm too-and that leads to less drama and more understanding.

A Little Humor Never Hurts

Let's be honest--staying calm all the time is easier said than done. There are moments when it's completely fine to throw your hands in the air and say, "I am not OK right now!" (and hey, we all have those moments). But here's the thing: even in those moments, humor can be a great ally. Laughter, after all, is one of the best ways to instantly release stress and bring calmness into a situation.

Ever had a bad day at work, and then something ridiculously silly happens that makes you crack up? That's your body's natural stress relief mechanism kicking in. So, next time life throws a curveball, try finding the humor in it even if it's just a little chuckle at how ridiculous this situation is. A smile, even a small one, can instantly reset your mood and help you approach challenges with a calmer mind.

At the end of the day calmness is a superpower! It isn't about eliminating stress-that's an impossible task. What it IS about is learning how to handle life's inevitable chaos with grace and poise. When you cultivate calmness, you gain control over your responses, improve your health, and foster more positive relationships.

When thrown off balance, remember: YOU and only YOU have the power to stay calm. Take the proverbial deep breath, shift your perspective, and maybe even share a laugh. As the saying goes, You've Got This!

***We don't stop playing because we get old.
We get old because we stop playing.***

3

Curiosity: The Spark That Starts Everything

Kids are naturally curious. They'll ask, "Why" until you lose the will to live! Adults, on the other hand, often stop asking. We settle into our routines, our habits, our favorite TV shows, and stop exploring like we've already seen the whole world.

Curiosity is the antidote to boredom. It's the difference between living on autopilot and living with awareness. Ask questions. Learn a new skill. Read weird articles that ordinarily wouldn't interest you. Try talking to someone whose life is nothing like yours.

You don't have to go full steam ahead, just get interested in something beyond your daily "To-Do" list. Curiosity makes you smarter, kinder, and infinitely more interesting at dinner parties!

How's this for example: Have you ever driven down the highway with a bug splattered windshield? You're squinting through dead bugs, mud, and that mysterious smear that only shows up at night under streetlights. You KNOW there's a clear road out there somewhere, but your view is half blocked, half guesswork, and you just HOPE you don't hit something... That's exactly what life feels like without CLARITY!

Clarity is the mental Windex we so badly need. It's the ability to see things as they really ARE--not as we fear they MIGHT be, (or WISH they were), but as they are right now, bugs and all!

When you can see clearly, suddenly everything gets easier. Decisions make more sense. Priorities line up. Confusion steps aside like a rude guest finally taking the hint at your dinner party.

But let's be real: clarity isn't always easy to come by. The world is noisy. Our minds are even noisier. Social media all around us is telling you what you SHOULD want... not what you DO want. There's family telling you what you OUGHT to do and your own brain whispering doubts at 3:00 in the morning when you're just trying to get a good night's sleep.

So, how do you clear the mental windshield that is in front of you and see where you're going?

Well, the good news is clarity isn't some mystical power only monks on mountain tops have. It takes practice. It's a skill. And like cleaning your car's windshield, you'll probably have to do it again and again, because life has a way of splattering bugs on your plans!

Why does clarity matter? It's the $1,000,000 question. Well for starters, confusion is exhausting! You know that feeling when you have fifty tabs open in your brain, half-finished projects, decisions you are intentionally avoiding, and questions you're too drained to answer.

That's called mental clutter, and like any hoarding situation, it eats up your energy like a Pac-Man with no regard for your personal sanity whatsoever!

Clarity does the opposite of this. When you get clear on what matters, you free up healthy mental space for the good stuff, AKA Focus, Creativity, and Confidence (hey, another "C" word)! You make far better decisions and spend less time guessing yourself, but most of all, you waste far less energy on things that don't deserve your attention.

Do you ever notice how a clear "yes" or "no" feels better than a wishy washy drawn out "maybe"? (I personally have an aversion to "maybe").

That's the power of clarity. That is that black hole that drags your focus into limbo. Clarity, on the other hand, sets you free.

What Gets in the Way?

So, if clarity is so wonderful, why do we lose it so easily and not make it a priority? Here are the most obvious reasons that in our hectic lives we seldom pay attention to enough. Here is your opportunity to turn chaos into not just clarity, but a life filled with organization and structure without becoming a robot!

- Overwhelmed: Too much to do, too many choices, too little time.... When you're overloaded, your brain's natural response is to fog up, (kinda like those bugs on the windshield).

- Noise: Social media, the nonstop addictive news, and other people's opinions can get so loud, you can't even hear your own thoughts.

- Fear: Clarity often asks for Honesty.... And honesty can often be one of the scariest things for people to deal with. What if the truth means you need to make a big change in your life? What if the answer isn't what you had hoped for? When we avoid looking too closely, which is the low hanging fruit as they say, the windshield stays dirty.

- Lack of reflection: We rarely pause long enough to ask, "What do I really want?" "What really matters?"

If you never stop, you never see beyond the foggy windshield.

Here lies the next question: How do we find clarity? How do we clear things up to promote concise clear thoughts that promote our joyous life?

Now for the good news! It's not difficult if you set your mind to it!

First and foremost, we must learn how to take out the Mental Trash.

We are going to start this with a Brain Dump.

Grab your notebook and pour out every thought swirling around in your head-your worries, your ideas, the to-dos, and any other half-baked plans swelling like a tornado in that brain of yours. Don't try to organize or make any judgment calls, just dump it all like you're emptying a junk drawer.

You will be amazed at how much mental clutter you're carrying around without even realizing. Once it's out, you can see it, and once you see it, you can deal with it. It's not so difficult when it's laid out in front of you.

Next, you're going to ask better questions to yourself. As funny as that sounds, YOU are your own best friend, and good questions are Clarity's best friend.

"What am I trying to do"?

"Why does it matter"?

"What's truly important here"?

And the big reveal and best one, "What would I tell a friend if they were in this situation?"

Weirdly enough, we often have great advice for others but can't see the obvious for ourselves. (Hump on a camel's back theory)!

Flip that around and be your own best friend.

None of this can be done without the limited-edition word, SILENCE. Clarity needs QUIET. Put down your phone. Take a walk. Turn off the TV, the podcast, the work stuff... be silent for fifteen minutes. Your brain won't like it and will try to resist and fill itself with random thoughts, but anything important will bubble up to the surface and allow you to rethink it.

Another oddity in relation to Clarity is the realization that you often need to decide not what you DO want in life, but what you DON'T want! This can be one of the hardest things for some people.

Most of us chase clarity by trying to figure out exactly what we want in life. But sometimes it's easier to start with what you realize you DON'T want.

What drains you? What do you keep doing out of habit, not necessarily out of desire? What are the things you secretly hate to do but do them anyway? Make a mental note every time you decide to eliminate the things, people, situations, or anything else that might muddy the waters. You'll realize that what remains is usually what you actually DO care about.

You realize as you get older, (again I say, trust me, I know), when in doubt, write it down. Your brain offers ideas without necessarily storing them all! Putting your thoughts on paper creates distance and allows you to not swim in confusion. We all lose clarity sometimes, even the people that write entire books about it.

Every morning you have a new opportunity to become a better version of yourself.

4

Why Commitment Matters

Commitment is the difference between a wish and a reality. It's what turns "maybe someday," into "look what I did!" It is showing up when you don't feel like it. Sticking with it when it's boring, and choosing it again and again, even when Netflix, your cozy bed, and a bowl of ice cream is calling your name!

You can have all the Calmness and Clarity in the world, (our first two C words), but without commitment, nothing sticks. Clarity gives you the map; commitment gets you in the car and keeps you driving when the road trip gets long and you're out of snacks!

Commitment doesn't care if you're motivated because motivation is fickle - here one day and ghosting you the next. Commitment will never ghost you. It's that reliable friend who shows up to help you move when everyone else suddenly “forgot.”

Commitment does not mean perfection. It’s not about being perfect, nor is it about never missing work or procrastinating. It's all about sticking with it anyway! Falling off the wagon, climbing back on and MOVING forward, where perfection says, “If I mess up, it's over.”

Commitment is saying, I screwed up. Now back to whatever I was doing and move forward.

Why do people struggle to stick with things that previously seemed so important? The two-word answer is: Immediate Gratification!!!

In this day and age, we have gotten spoiled, and we expect instant results! This modern life has trained us to want everything... NOW! From 2-day shipping, which now feels like 'ground' lol, to same-day groceries, DoorDash, even instant noodles are now a reality. But what most people don't like to hear is that REAL change takes time.

Commitment means trusting the process when the results seem invisible if not darn right intangible.

We rely on the initial motivation, which is great for starters, but not so great at sticking around.

That is when commitment kicks in.

Commitment kicks in when motivation checks out!

Between this computerized world, and our obsession with instant gratification, we easily get distracted. Usually, new, shiny things look better than old, tired ones, and tease our minds into losing focus on the things we've already chosen. Commitment asks you to look away from the shiny objects and realign your mindset.

Another ginormous reason people are afraid of commitment is the ever-nagging Fear of Failure! Back to, "The devil you know is better than the devil you *don't* know" concept. "What if we try it, and it doesn't work?" Well, keep in mind if you don't try at all, you fail either way!

The fact about commitment is that it's better to fail trying than fail by default!

So, where do we start in our quest to build real commitment when it is so important for a grounded self-fulfilled life? Here's the good news... commitment isn't ONLY about willpower. It's about learning to stick with it by making that commitment EASIER than QUITTING!

A commitment doesn't need to be a giant heroic feat. Those often backfire, as they can feel impossible to achieve. But instead, make tiny commitments that you build on. Practice in anything you try, makes one become more proficient, until it miraculously becomes second nature!

Ready for the 'secret sauce'? Here's how it's done!

Do you want to start to read more? Commit to only ten minutes a day and build up from there.

Do you want to get fit? Commit to walking for ten minutes and build up to 1/2 hour if not an hour a day.

Do you want to write a book? (I know this one!) Commit to writing 200 words a day and watch how the words begin to pour out of you!

Tiny small steps are sustainable. Seeds grow into giant trees. Same thing with our process on learning to keep commitments.

Another way to become Commitment enriched is to make it obvious. Most people do not want to talk about their commitments for the fear of not following through. If your commitment is known only to you, it is easy to either forget it existed in the first place or not follow through.

Do you want to eat healthier? Buy healthy foods and put them in clear sight. Then tell people what your new health commitment is and how you plan to achieve it. The ones that care about you will be happy to help you reach your goal and not sabotage your good intentions.

Habits consistently outperform willpower. To make your commitment stick, turn it into a behavior you automatically do already. That's how real progress becomes effortless. For example, if you would like to do something as simple as drinking more water (which we are all told is important), put water next to something you regularly do. Putting it near your toothbrush or next to your laptop or anything else that you naturally do every day will remind you to drink it and make it easier to follow through with your commitment. Now wasn't that easy?

Don't beat yourself up if you miss a day or even a week. That can be the number one motivation killer. Self-kindness and self-compassion can be just the thing to prevent your losing motivation and can be just the thing you need to revive your commitment!

Commitment isn't just for goals, and if anything, most people associate the word *commitment* with relationships. Commitment is the heart of healthy relationships.

Showing up for loved ones, friends, or coworkers, even when it's inconvenient, shows respect and commitment. The hardest one of all these days could be staying PRESENT, when it's easier to scroll down your phone. (OK who's done that, raise your hand).

Choosing to REALLY listen when you'd rather defend or explain yourself... Commitment is the glue that holds friendships, families, and partnerships together.

We all know that person who flakes the moment something better comes along. DON'T BE THAT PERSON.

Be the one that shows up. Be the one people trust to mean it when they say, "I'm there for you."

Some people are better at committing to others than they are to themselves. That can be tricky, as it's a fine line between committing yourself and losing yourself to everything and everyone around you, just to be a people pleaser. Watch that slippery slope! Constantly cancelling things, i.e., skipping the workout, dropping the project, postponing your dreams, means you are not worth showing up for. The promises you make to yourself matter just as much as the ones you make to others, if not more. So, keeping those promises even the small ones, or I should say, especially the small ones, must take priority.

Commitment and Flexibility

Commitment doesn't mean rigid stubbornness. Sometimes the thing you commit to NEEDS to change, and that's okay. As I always say, not everything is set in stone... except maybe a tombstone, lol. (Oh, come on, finding humor in almost everything is a gift.)

Always remember that staying committed to your values is far more important than sticking to a goal that no longer fits.

If your plan isn't working the way you had intended, then tweak the plan-it doesn't mean you have to abandon commitment to your bigger vision, it only means that your original intention needs updating.

Sometimes the bravest commitment is just walking away from something that is not serving you. A job that drains your soul, a habit that's hurting you, or a goal that you may have chosen for the wrong reason, even a person that has worn out their welcome so to speak! This is why you should think through things seriously and never feel guilty rehashing or reconsidering commitment if it just doesn't feel right.

Making a commitment doesn't mean you are stuck forever. It means staying true to what matters MOST. And sometimes, that means saying GOODBYE so you can say YES to something that is meaningful and aligns with your goals and value system better.

Commitment feels good because it is also freedom in a sense. It is putting your good energy into something that you choose that makes you feel good inside. When you commit to something, you stop wasting energy and you do it with gumption and compassion.

In the end, commitment is simple:

*Choose what matters.

*Show up for it.

*Repeat!

No perfection required!!! What a Concept!

No magic, no shortcuts--just the kind of everyday commitment that makes the life you want not just POSSIBLE, but DOABLE and REAL!

In order to attain the impossible, one must attempt the absurd.

5

Creativity: It's in ALL of us

Creativity is the word which unleashes the magic in everyday life! It is the magic we have in each and every one of us. That little spark and secret ingredient that turns the ordinary into extraordinary! But somehow, the moment we hear the word *creativity*, we tend to picture the paint splattered artist covered in bright colors, hunched over a canvas deep in thought, waiting for a flash of divine inspiration.

But here's the unknown secret: CREATIVITY is not just reserved for artists or genius inventors! It is for all of us! It's in every idea, every problem we solve, and in every quirky solution to a challenge. It's what makes life a little or a lot more fun. It's what creates excitement in everyday life. It IS in every one of us and not just some rare gift that only a select few get to enjoy.

Creativity involves taking the leftovers in the freezer and turning them into an exciting dinner. It's about taking a ho-hum weekend and turning it into an adventure! It's about making every day feel like Disney World! We all can do it: it is allowing ourselves the freedom with the help of our old best friend "Courage" to allow us to be spontaneous and our other handy friend 'Commitment' to help us have the "Chutzpa" to try something new!

Let's imagine a life without creativity, (although you may already have that now)! No new ideas, no new solutions to problems, no innovative ways of making things easier or more fun and festive. Sounds boring, right?? Well, it IS!

Creativity makes life more colorful. It says 'Adios' to the dull and boring. It takes black and white television into cinematic colorful TV! It helps us navigate more smoothly through the tough stuff. (So, what's the downside?!)

When life throws challenges at you, Creativity is what lets you bend and adapt to replace bruises and scratches. It's what helps you find new paths when the old ones become blocked. It's what gives you the ability as well as the STABILITY to see the possibility in every situation-even when it seems like there's no hope.

Without creativity, we are stuck. We'd stick to the same routines, think the same thoughts, and do the same things repeatedly, mostly without even thinking! Now, ADD creativity into the mix, and we are free to invent new ways of thinking, living, and being! Woot Woot!!

Creativity is all around us, so let's explore how creativity shows up in our life, in our everyday encounters and how we can recognize it.

Creativity is when you figure out how to finish that project at work with minimal resources. It is solving problems with whatever you have at hand and feeling a sense of accomplishment when you do it. It is the delicious new recipe you come up with using whatever you find in the fridge! It is navigating tricky situations with humor, grace, and a lot of improvisation. It is the ability to adapt on the fly when other people throw their hands in the air with frustration. For that matter, it is the reason that people gravitate to creative people!

Why is that person surrounded with a flock of admirers that seem so intrigued just being around their presence, while someone else is sitting miserable like a bump on a log?

The obvious is that a creative person is INTERESTING. The creative person sees life in general through a different lens, always looking for a more interesting approach. The mundane turns into excitement for them. For them, the kaleidoscope is more fun than the telescope!

Don't believe the pervasive myth that only certain people are creative--the ones who are born with the 'gift,' who can write symphonies or paint the Mona Lisa. Don't let that short-sighted thought process stifle your desire to be creative. The truth is, EVERYONE has creativity within them! It's just a matter of recognizing it and nurturing it.

With the belief, that the creative genius is the man behind the curtain keeps you from exploring your own creativity. You think you're just not good enough or artistic enough, but here is the reality: creativity is about SOLVING problems, not just making art. It's about thinking differently whether you're tackling a work challenge, coming up with a fun family activity, or brainstorming ways to improve your daily routine.

So, let's crush that myth right now. Creativity isn't about being the painter or the poet; it's about being an analytical person, an improviser, and an inventor in your own life.

Creativity is not something that fades as we grow older as one might think. When that happens, it is our own prejudices of being afraid to think freely that hold us back from having a more fun exciting life.

As children, we draw, build, and make things just for the fun of it. But somewhere along the way, we stopped. The world subliminally tells us that creativity is only for artists, so we let it go. We grow more focused on the results than the process. We think we need to be serious, and that's when creativity gets shoved to the side. But here is the thing; it's not something you need to grow out of. In fact, creativity might be more important NOW than ever. When we STOP being creative, we stop thinking outside the box. We lose the ability to adapt, to innovate, and to take risks. The more we 'Grow Up' in the traditional sense, the more we risk shutting down our creativity?

The truth is that the world needs your creative spark now more than ever.

How to Unlock Your Creativity

If you are ready and willing to bring creativity into your life or perhaps BACK into your life, here's how you do it!

- Give Yourself Permission to Play

We get so caught up in doing things right and the way society expects us to do them, that we forget to have fun. But creativity thrives on play. When was the last time you did something just because it felt good, with no agenda or end goal? Whether it's doodling, daydreaming, or making up silly songs in the shower, creativity comes alive when we let go of perfectionism and give ourselves permission to play.

Don't stress out about being good at it. Just do it. Play, explore, and experiment. That's when the magic happens!

- Making Time for Exploring

Creativity needs time and space to grow. The problem is, we're all busy, but guess what? Creativity doesn't need hours of your time; it just needs moments of curiosity.

Take five minutes a day to explore something new. Try a new hobby. Try new food. Read an article on a subject you know nothing about but always found intriguing. Watch a television show or documentary in a completely different genre than you usually gravitate towards. Let your brain wander into uncharted territory. You'll be surprised how much creativity grows when you give it some freedom and permission.

- Find Inspiration Everywhere

From the books you read, the conversations you have, the places you visit or anything else that sparks your interest. Whether in nature or the people you meet every day, let your thoughts go a little rogue and have fun with them. Stop looking for creativity in only the perfect moments. Let ordinary, everyday situations spark new ideas. Pay attention to the small things that make you laugh, think, or just wonder. Those are the seeds of true creativity.

- Let Yourself Fail

It sounds counterintuitive, but sometimes the best way to be creative is to fail. We all know creativity requires risk. It's about trying something new and yes, sometimes failing but failing isn't the end all; it's part of the process. Every failure teaches you something new, something that will make your next attempt or adventure even better. Don't let fear or failure keep you from being creative. Embrace your mistakes and learn from them. After all, even Picasso had some terrible paintings!

- Create without Judgment

This one's a big one: stop judging your ideas before you even start. Creativity needs freedom to flow and that means letting go of your inner critic which can be the worst one of them all. The more you criticize yourself, the more you shut down your creativity.

Instead, create freely. Let your ideas flow without worrying about what anyone else will think. Who cares? As long as you are not hurting anyone in the process, be free, have fun and you will be amazed at the new energy you have and those that want to be around you! The more you do this, the more creative you will become.

Closing Thoughts to mull over... You are ALREADY CREATIVE!

At the end of the day, creativity isn't something you have to go out searching for. It's already within you. It's in how you solve problems, how you express yourself, and how you find joy in the little moments. Creativity is part of being human, and the more you embrace it, the more it will grow. So go ahead-play. Experiment. Fail. Dream. Create. The world needs your unique spark, and the more you let it shine, the brighter it will make your life!

Challenges are simply new opportunities.

6

Building Strength Through Long-Term Struggles

Having resilience in the face of the long haul of challenges is not an easy task. Yes, life is full of challenges, but some of them stick around longer than others. They don't just pass in a few days or weeks. These are the struggles that hang around, testing your patience and your spirit, AKA the CHRONIC ones... the Chronic illness, Chronic stress, Chronic uncertainty. They can all feel like a never-ending battle, a long haul with no clear end in sight.

But here's the truth: these long-term struggles are not just obstacles to endure. They are life opportunities to build something stronger than we ever thought possible: RESILIENCE.

When life tests you day in and day out, you're not just surviving-you're becoming something more. Something more capable of withstanding the storms of life. Navigating these ongoing challenges with strength, grace, and determination. Here's the key to dealing with chronic struggles. They shouldn't be something that we just push through-they are something we can GROW through. And while they may change us, they don't have to DEFINE us.

Why chronic struggles are different is because they take us down the long road. Short-term struggles are just a basic part of life; we all face them. A difficult conversation, an unexpected setback, or just a bad day at work. They're like storms that pass quickly. But chronic struggles? They're like heavy rain that doesn't ever seem to let up. You can't just wait for them to pass; you must figure out how to live with the downpour, and how to adapt to the steady never-ending drizzle of challenges that persist over time.

Chronic struggles come in many forms, but they all have one main thing in common: they test our ability to endure. They push us to the brink, forcing us to dig deeper than we ever have before. And because these struggles last, they can make us feel stuck like we're treading water in an endless sea.

But the difference between just SURVIVING and THRIVING through chronic struggles is this: our RESPONSE.

When we choose to face these long -term challenges with a mindset of growth, we transform the whole experience. No, the struggle doesn't disappear, but we learned to meet it with strength and resilience, building a foundation of power that we didn't even know we had. This is the reward that we weren't expecting. (Remember, we are always trying to find that silver lining in the black cloud; so here it is)!

So, how do we build strength when the fight seems endless? How do we turn chronic challenges into opportunities for growth?

It all starts with your perspective.

- Embrace this Struggle as part of your life's story.

What does that mean?

We often look at our struggles as something to just get rid of, something to endure until they pass. But what if we could see them as part of our story, woven into the fabric of who we are and what made us the person we are today?

Instead of pushing them away or ignoring their impact, we can choose to embrace them. This doesn't mean we have to love our struggles, but we can acknowledge them as part of our life's journey.

Think about it this way: the strongest trees on earth don't grow in perfect conditions. They grow through storms, their roots spreading deeper thicker and stronger as they fight to stay upright. The same way, our struggles can deepen our roots. Our understanding and capacity for resilience grows under this pressure and conditions.

- Accepting what you can't control.

One of the most difficult aspects of chronic struggles is the feeling of powerlessness. When you're dealing with a long-term illness, a difficult family situation, or the common ongoing financial stress, it can feel like you have no control and no way to turn. The more you fight against what's beyond your control, the more frustrated and exhausted you become.

Building strength in the face of chronic struggles requires us to let go of what we can't control and focus on what we CAN control. We can control our attitude for sure. We can control our actions and our response to what is happening. This shift in mindset doesn't make the struggle easier, but what it does is give you the power to navigate it in a way that feels more empowering.

- Cultivate patience and persistence.

Strength doesn't come overnight, and like a habit, it's built through repetition. Couple that with persistence (and a lot of patience), and you may find it showing up day after day, even when things aren't getting any easier. The power of chronic struggle is in the long game. It is in continuing to push forward even when you're not sure when things will change.

Think about the marathon runner who trains for months, running mile after mile, with no finish line insight. But every step, every effort, is building their strength. Even when the race feels long and exhausting, every mile conquered is another victory!

- The power of routine and ritual

When you're facing a chronic struggle, the unpredictability of the situation can create a sense of mental chaos. This is where you must create routines and rituals. You must create a sense of structure and consistency in your day, even when everything around you feel uncertain.

What we also know is that chronic struggles can make us feel like we're constantly failing because we don't see immediate results. We all like instant gratification, but chronic struggles defy those odds. The key is to focus on the small wins. What can you do today that will move you forward, even just a little? Celebrate those victories. They really matter. They're building this strength, even if it feels like it's a slow process.

A small win could be something as simple as taking a walk, writing down one positive thing that happened today, or having a conversation that makes you feel connected. These wins may seem insignificant in the grand scheme of things, but they are going to be what keeps you going when the struggle feels endless.

Through all this, self-care is the most essential luxury you can afford yourself. If you don't like the word LUXURY in the face of chronic struggle, let's change it to Necessity! Taking care of your physical, emotional, and mental health is crucial in building the strength you need to keep going.

Make time for practices that nourish you-whether it's meditation, writing in a journal, taking a warm bath, or adopting a hobby that brings you joy.

The power of routine and ritual is that they create a needed sense of stability in your life. Even on the hardest days, you can find comfort in the things that help you feel more grounded, safe, and worthy. Piggybacking this with a good support system is also self-care. You don't need to face chronic struggles alone. One of the greatest sources of strength can come from the people around you... friends, family, support groups, or even a therapist can offer comfort, encouragement, and practical help when you need it most.

Because support is a two-way street, there's a unique power that comes from shared struggles. As you lean on others, be sure to offer your support when they need it as well: it deepens connections and reminds us that we are never truly alone.

To sum it up, when you face a long-term challenge, it's easy to allow it to define you. "I am sick," "I am overwhelmed," "I am failing." But here's the key: Life is so much more than what you are facing. Never let the struggle take over every aspect of your identity which is easier said than done. Yes, you may be facing a chronic illness or an ongoing hardship, but that doesn't mean you are weak or incapable. In fact, the very fact that you continue to show up to deal with this every day speaks to your strength and determination.

You're not shaped by the challenges you face—but by the way you rise to meet them. How you choose to respond, and how you choose to keep moving forward, even when it feels and seems impossible, is the defining moment. The most resilient people in the world are those who maintain HOPE, even when everything around them seems uncertain.

Remember, it's not about pretending things are fine when they aren't. On the contrary, it's about believing that, even if things are hard now, there IS a way forward.

It's about trusting that this struggle will not last forever, and that better days are surely possible even if you can't see them yet!

No one is perfect - that's why pencils have erasers.

7

Contentment: The Joy Inside Us

Picture this: you're sitting in your favorite safe spot, enjoying your favorite beverage in hand, and surprisingly, nothing pressing on your To-Do List. The world outside may be bustling, but at this moment, you feel an incredible deep sense of peace. This serene state, free from the constant chase for more, is what is known as Contentment.

Contentment is not complacency - it's far from that. It's about finding joy and real, honest satisfaction in the present moment, regardless of any external circumstances.

It's recognizing that happiness doesn't always have to come from achieving "the next big thing," but from embracing what we already have in our lives.

Imagine a world where we celebrate the little moments-where a quiet morning, a hearty laugh with friends, or a peaceful sunset becomes the highlight of the day. Contentment invites us to find joy in those moments. To find joy in the present, appreciating the beauty of what we have right now.

Most people do not know how to cultivate contentment in their lives. They don't realize that sometimes it takes a commitment to themselves to have it and practice it until it becomes a habit. The key to contentment is to focus not on what's LACKING in your life, but what is ABUNDANT in your life.

One of the most effective ways to foster contentment is by practicing gratitude. The best way to do this each day is to take a few minutes to write down things you are grateful for. This practice of acknowledging these blessings shifts your focus organically!

Learn the concept of mindful living

Mindfulness is about being fully present in the moment. Whether you're eating, walking, or spending time with loved ones, savor each experience. Mindful living helps you appreciate life's simple pleasures and cultivates a sense of contentment. A big part of this is learning how to limit comparisons.

With a world of social media highlight reels, it's easy to fall into the trap of comparing ourselves to others. Instagram, Facebook, and all the other life exposing outlets make it difficult to not compare ourselves to others. Remember that everyone's journey is unique. Focus on your own progress and achievements.

Celebrate your milestones, no matter how small they seem to you.

In relation to that, you must embrace simplicity. Simplifying your life can lead to greater contentment. Clutter invades both your physical space and mental load. Focus on what truly matters and let go of the excess. It doesn't mean you have to give up everything you love; it's about finding balance and joy in simplicity, a lot harder than it seems, but doable.

Contentment isn't about giving up on your goals or your dreams; It's about finding a balance. It's perfectly fine to strive for more, but it's equally important to pause and appreciate where you are right now. It is a fine line between ambition and gratitude. When we allow ourselves to be content, we create space for joy, creativity, and a deeper appreciation for life's journey.

Often waiting for big milestones before we allow ourselves to feel proud, we forget to celebrate the small wins. The truth is, genuine contentment often comes from the quiet victories—not the ones that get applause, but the ones that shape your everyday joy. Did you make it through an impossible frustrating week at work without quitting or losing your coolness? Celebrate that! Did you manage to stick to your exercise routine for a few days? High five to you! These small victories are the Secret building blocks of contentment. They remind us that we're making progress, even if it doesn't always feel like it.

Perfection is the ultimate contentment killer. It keeps you focused on what's NOT right, preventing you from appreciating what IS! *Spoiler alert*: embrace the idea that things don't have to be perfect to be wonderful!

That perfect meal, that slightly messy house, the unpolished presentation - they all add up to the charm of life. Letting go of perfection opens a big space for joy and that's where its contentment thrives!

Spending time with positive people can greatly influence our sense of contentment. Positive, supportive individuals help create an environment where we feel good if not great about ourselves and our lives. On the flip side, negative energy drains us. Try to surround yourself with people who lift you up, and inspire you, and whenever possible, surround yourself with people that make you laugh! That energy will rub off on you, making contentment feel a lot more natural.

My favorite of all and what I find the easiest of all is engaging in acts of kindness. Helping others doesn't just improve your day, it can also boost your own sense of contentment by default. Whether it's volunteering, lending a hand to a friend, or simply offering a smile to a stranger, acts of kindness connect us to others and remind us of the goodness in the world so easily forgotten. When we do something kind, we often feel a deep sense of fulfillment that can never be found in material pursuits.

The bottom line here is contentment is not a destination, but a journey. It's the practice of showing up each day, doing your best, and appreciating what you have in the moment. It's about being okay with where you are and who you are, without the constant need to chase more or be better. And, as we've explored, contentment doesn't have to be complicated. In fact, it could be one of the easiest things to achieve. It's found in the little things-the joy of the morning cup of coffee, or in my case, the coffee and the acai bowl, The peace of a quiet evening watching Netflix, or just the warmth of good natural conversation with friends.

In the end, contentment allows us to live more Fulfilled. When we stop waiting for the perfect moment or the next big achievement to feel happy, we open ourselves up to the beauty of life as it exists. So, take a deep breath, appreciate where you are, and let yourself savor the present!

A man's character is his fate.

8

The Charm of Change

What do we do when life throws a curveball?

Change is the thing we claim to want and secretly hope stays politely at the door. We always hear the expressions "Change is the only constant" or "Be the change you wish to see." That all sounds like Gandhi is talking to you from above, lovely, and inspiring. But when it knocks on our door, we tend to try to hide from it.

Change doesn't always show up with fireworks and big announcements. Sometimes it sneaks in quietly-a new job, a new friendship, a small shift in how you see the world. Sometimes it crashes in uninvited – a breakup, a move, an unexpected challenge. Sometimes we choose it-sometimes bravely, sometimes foolishly, but most of the time hopefully. However, it arrives, change always brings the gift of growth whether you ask for it or not.

So, getting comfortable with the uncomfortable is what I call it. Let's talk about how to not just survive change but to also welcome it like an old friend, who occasionally overstays their welcome, but usually has a good story to go along with it!

Why do we fear change and why it's OK....

First things first: if change freaks you out, congratulations, you are human! Our brains crave certainty. We love patterns, predictability, and the safety of "the known." In modern life, when change looms--even GOOD changes--our minds whisper, "Danger! Unknown territory! Run!"

Understanding this natural behavioral concept helps us be kinder to ourselves when it comes to change. You're not weak for feeling anxious about change, you're just - NORMAL!

The goal isn't to Never feel fear--it's to move through it anyway with at least anxiety as possible.

Let's face it, not all change is dramatic. However, sometimes it's the little things that shift us the most. Small changes add up. They're gentle nudges that lead us to bigger shifts: whether it's more energy, more presence, or more intention, big changes often start with a tiny decision that maybe even felt like nothing at the time.

Now let's deal with the reality of the big ones, AKA the tidal waves of change. The move across the country, the total career change, the unexpected, or even the expected, end of a relationship or even the beginning of a new one. Or it could be the health change that sends you into a tizzy and makes you rethink everything in your life from start to finish.

Big change demands courage and courage doesn't mean not being scared. It means being scared and doing it anyway. It's about packing up the boxes, sending the application, or having that hard conversation when your knees are shaking so badly you think people can hear them.

When these big shifts come, remind yourself: I've done this before.... Because you have. You've survived every change that life has thrown you so far, even the ones you swore you wouldn't survive, which is proof you can do it again!

The secret to dancing with grace when it comes to change is knowing when to let go of the past version of you that doesn't fit anymore, or the habits that drag you down to be a person you don't like anymore. The relationship that drains you or the dream that no longer sparks joy in your life. Reminding yourself that letting go is not failure and if anything, it's wisdom. It's the brave art of making space for what's next.

Letting go does not leave you with emptiness--it leaves you with your next possibility!

Your new best friend Uncertainty!

Change and uncertainty are best friends. They show up together, whether we like it or not. The trick here is becoming friends with the uncertainty, replacing demanding answers with open questions. Instead of clinging to the plan, stay curious about what's around the corner. It's a mindset shift from, "What if this goes wrong" to "What if this goes better than I could even imagine"?!

We all know we can't control everything, but what we do know, is we can choose how we meet the unknown - with clenched fists, or open arms.

Thc best part is finding fun in change!

Some changes are genuinely hard, that's a Gimme. Not all change is going to be good. None of us are that blind or have our heads in the clouds that high. But even then, try to find tiny sparks of humor or create an adventure through it all. If you are moving to a new city, starting a new job, or getting out of a relationship, you have a chance to learn, grow, and reinvent yourself. Yes, it's an unexpected detour, but it will turn into a story to tell later and hopefully a funny one!

Your homework for today:

Tips for Thriving and Surviving Through Change

Let's wrap this up with some practical, down-to-earth ways to navigate change with a little more grace --and maybe even a smile!

STAY ANCHORED:

When life seems like a whirlwind, holding tightly to your anchors-daily routine is important. Trusted friends are just as important. Stick to your small rituals that ground you.

TALK IT OUT:

Share your fears, your hopes and your even wild, “What-If’s” with people who listen without judgment... (That last word is important).

STAY FLEXIBLE:

Plans are great –until they're not! Stay open to adjusting as you go.

CELEBRATE PROGRESS:

Don't wait until you've “figured it all out"-celebrate every brave step you take, even if it seems silly.

And mostly... BE PATIENT!

Some changes take time, a lot of time. Revealing the gift of change can often take a lot of unfolding or peeling back the onion. Trust the process and go with the flow.

Here's what I hope you will take from this chapter: CHANGE is NOT YOUR ENEMY. It is an invitation to grow, to evolve, and to become a version of yourself you haven't met yet, but I think you will like it. So next time change knocks on your door, don't hide behind the curtains. Open the door. Offer it a welcome beverage and ask what it can teach you. Because in the end, life is all about change. When we learn to accept the inevitable as natural, we truly learn to live!

It's amazing what you can accomplish if you don't care who gets the credit.

9

The Art of Building, Not Breaking

There's something quietly powerful about the word CONSTRUCTIVE. It doesn't shout like ambitious or glitter like charismatic. It doesn't storm into a room like Confidence. But make no mistake, it's the solid scaffolding that holds all those 'C' words together! To be constructive means to build. To contribute. To add something good where nothing existed or where something broken needed mending.

It's the hammer and nails in a world full of demolition crews and wrecking balls.

If you've ever worked with a true problem solver, you know what constructive energy feels like. They don't roll their eyes or shrug off an obstacle. They lean in, sleeves up, asking, "What can we do about it?" and "How do we make this happen"? You walk away a little lighter and feel confident that this person has got this. Because constructive people don't just TELL you what's wrong they help you figure it out and work at making it right.

Constructive isn't just "think happy thoughts and ignore reality." That's not helpful and frankly, it's annoying. There's a huge difference between blind positivity ("Everything's fine, no worries!") And true constructive thinking ("Things are a mess – let's fix them.")

Constructive people see the cracks, but they bring the mortar, so to speak. They see the conflict, but they offer a solution. They don't stick their heads in the sand, and on the contrary, they dig their hands into the soil and plant something better.

Most of us dip into destructive thinking more than we'd like to admit because it's easier. Destructive mindsets don't build anything- they just clear the ground and leave it barren. But here's the good news: if you can be DE-structive, you can also be CON-structive! Think of it this way, it takes the same energy, just aimed in a different direction! If you have the power to tear something down, you have the power to build it up!

So where do we start? Well, where do all your best (as well as worst), projects begin? In your own head! Think of your thoughts as your blueprint! If your blueprint is sloppy, your building won't stand for long. If your blueprint is meticulous, flexible, and hopeful, your mind becomes a workshop for good things.

Constructive thinking is about catching yourself and those destructive loops and asking yourself "Is this thought helping me build or tear down?"

When you don't have the confidence to take the bull by the horns, you lay down a weak foundation for self-doubt. When you have good and strong intentions to create something with gusto and mind strength, you're not sugarcoating reality; you are just framing a doorway for improvement!

Turn your inner criticism into constructive criticism. What can I do instead to make this better? Always look for the upside in every situation. Constructive thinking isn't about pretending everything is always fine. It's about keeping the hammer in your hand instead of throwing it across the room!

Now that we've covered how to be constructive inside your own head, let's talk about how to carry that blueprint into your personal relationships.

Let's face it, the world is full of people who can always find flaws. Anyone can point out what's broken. The real magic in life is in helping fix it.

The most obvious place where we build or break things or relationships is with our words. The tongue can be a constructive word or a destructive word. It's free and easy to use, but most people don't think about the consequences of their words. Words are like tools – some people swing them around like a sledgehammer or whack away at you like a chisel, but the goal of being constructive is to carve, shape, and support, not to smash everything to pieces.

Think about the last time someone gave you feedback. Was it helpful? Encouraging? Or did it leave you feeling defensive, embarrassed, or small? Constructive feedback doesn't tiptoe around the truth but delivers the truth with respect, care, and the genuine desire to help. Constructive speech builds trust. Destructive speech tears down confidence. Why would anybody want to do that to somebody?

Being constructive doesn't mean being a doormat or sugar coating everything until it becomes meaningless. Sometimes being constructive means saying something difficult but saying it in a way that opens a door instead of slamming it in your face.

You know those conversations that you dread? Things that keep you up all night? Maybe it's telling your friend how they've hurt you. Maybe it's giving honest feedback to a friend or colleague. Maybe it's setting a boundary that's long overdue.

A destructive approach to tough talk usually involves blame, shame, or explosions. A constructive approach involves curiosity, clarity, and kindness. Like all the other chapters about the wonderful 'C' words in the English language, they all seem so obvious. But focusing on words and how they affect not just you, but those around you, is a great way to live a positive happy life! Incorporating these beautiful words into your life—not just to spark creation, but to sustain the kind of life you thought only the lucky enjoyed isn't a privilege for a chosen few. It's a powerful gift you choose to give yourself. Here's a little 'cheat sheet' to help you be a more constructive human being:

- START WITH PURPOSE

"I'm bringing this up because I care about this project/relationship."

- USE "I" STATEMENT

"I felt frustrated when... " instead of, "you always."

- FOCUS FORWARD

"How can we fix this?" instead of "You Aways..." or "Look what you did."

The use of constructive encouragement is one of the most underrated superpowers we have. Real encouragement is specific, sincere, and timely. Encouragement builds people up brick by brick. Over time, it creates a foundation of trust and motivation that keeps teams together, friendships solid, and families close. It doesn't cost anything as we said before, and yet, it is priceless! Give it out generously and watch the unexpected return!

On the flip side, being constructive means more than just THINKING good thoughts or SAYING helpful things; it's about doing something with that energy. This is where a lot of well-meaning people get stuck. They are professionals at pointing out what's wrong, they can talk about the solutions for hours, but when it's time to act, they're suddenly "too busy" or "not ready yet."

When this happens, remember the hard truth: ideas are cheap and easy. Action is the currency that builds real things that don't collapse when the wind blows!

Being constructive consists of being able to solve problems instead of just complaining. Let's admit it, we all love a good vent session or bitch session! However, a little complaining can be healthy when it lets off steam. But there's a thin line between venting and getting stuck in a swamp of negativity.

Constructive people are aware of how they think and notice when they're complaining about the same problem for days or weeks. That's when they decide to build a bridge out of it, instead of being a rat on a treadmill.

So next time you catch yourself in a complaint loop like the little rat, pause and ask yourself: "What exactly am I frustrated about?"

"What small action can I take to improve this right now?"

"Who could I ask for help or ideas that will be an asset and not a Debbie or Danny downer?"

From there, here is another secret. Many great ideas are born out of pure annoyance! Many businesses, books, and inventions are born out of frustration—when someone decides that the way things are just isn't good enough and chooses to create something better. Instead of throwing up their hands, they rolled up their sleeves!

Being constructive means using frustration as the fuel, not fire. As they say, you don't burn down the whole house to fix drafty windows!

It may not be easy to live your life in what may appear to be a fantasy world of hope; in fact, it may seem downright exhausting. The world can be a negative place, critical and dismissive. Don't allow your mind to give up and practice these little tricks that we spoke about earlier. You could be the most constructive person on earth, but if you surround yourself with cynical, energy- sucking vampires, they will try to bulldoze your work and good intentions.

You can't change everyone, but you surely can change how you respond. Make clear boundaries, limit exposure where you can, encounter destructive talk with gentle but firm redirection. Remind yourself that even the most constructive people have days when they think, "What's the point, nothing ever changes."

That's normal.

The difference is they don't live in that space. They vent; they take a break and then pick up all the tools that help them have a better tomorrow and move on!

Constructive people also understand sometimes you must start fresh, and they are brave enough to do it with a plan. They understand that sometimes demolition is necessary, and some things must come down to rebuild something better. They don't cling to dead weight. They don't let life get them down or obstructions get in their way. They either move them or go around them, but they figure it out, and you can, too.

Being constructive is about more than just having a good attitude. It's about leaving things better than you find them, whether it be in your mind, your relationships, or even your community.

Destructive people are loud. They get attention. But constructive people get things done! They build families that last, businesses that grow, and friendships that heal communities that thrive. They are the quiet carpenters of a better world. So, next time you're tempted to tear down, pause, pick up your fictitious hammer and ask, "What can I build here instead?"

One thought, one word, one action at a time – now that's how you make a life that's truly constructive!

You're allowed to pause but never quit.

10

The Quiet Strength that Speaks FOR You

Character isn't flashy. It doesn't walk into a room ahead of you, dressed in confidence or charisma. It doesn't shout. It doesn't sell. But it DOES speak!

It speaks through your choices.

It speaks through how you treat people when there's nothing to gain.

It speaks when you keep your word – especially when it's inconvenient.

And it speaks even louder when no one is watching.

If confidence is how you feel about yourself, character is how you behave regardless of how you feel.

We live in a world that often rewards image over substance, speed over steadiness, performance over principle. And yet, character remains the bedrock of real trust, real respect, and real relationships.

In this chapter, we're not just talking about "being a good person." We're talking about what holds you together when life shakes you. What people remember about you when you're not in the room. What builds trust with others and peace within yourself - the added bonus, so to speak.

We're talking about the quiet strength that outlasts charm. We're talking about CHARACTER!

The two pillars of character are trust and consistency. People often say, "Trust is earned." And that's true.

But they leave out the part about HOW it's earned – through CONSISTENCY.

Not perfection. Not grand gestures. Just steady, repeatable integrity. For example, when someone says they'll show up and they do, time after time-you trust them.

When someone listens without judgment and keeps your confidence – you trust them. When someone admits when they're wrong and corrects it – you trust them.

That's character in action. It's not about one shining moment of decency. It's all about the pattern. The quiet reliability that tells people, I am who I say I am. Sadly, this trait is not as common as it should be, but luckily for you, it makes people with character stand out from the crowd!

When your actions align with your values, not just occasionally, but habitually, your sense of self grows stronger. Your inner critic quiets. This happens because you are not performing a role, you're showing up as yourself. Because character isn't built from comfort, it's easy to appear principled when everything is going well. When you are restored, appreciated, and things are in your favor. But character doesn't develop in easy moments. It shows up in the hard ones.

True character is forged not by perfection, but by the courage to admit mistakes instead of hiding them. When you do the right thing, even when no one would know otherwise. When you stay calm in chaos, as well as kind in conflict. And lastly, when you choose humility over ego.

These aren't always dramatic moments. Sometimes character is tested by the smallest choices: how you speak to a waitress or cashier, whether you choose to gossip or stay quiet when it's so tempting to do otherwise. And how do you handle frustration when things don't go your way? The truth is that character is born out of the fire of discomfort. You don't need a crisis to build it, but challenges will certainly reveal it.

One of the biggest myths is that character is something you either have, or you don't. But character is not a fixed trait; it's practice. It's shaped by intention and strengthened by repetition and if anything, character reveals itself over time.

You CAN build character at any point in your life, so don't despair! You can also RE-build character because no one gets it right all the time. Not one of us can say we haven't made choices that we regret. We all fall short of our own standards as well as other people's. This doesn't disqualify you from being a person of character, it just gives you the opportunity to have it! What matters in life is how you respond!

Do you take responsibility?

Do you try to make it right?

Do you LEARN from it and grow?

The strongest people of character are often the ones who've failed, owned it, and risen with more compassion and self-awareness.

What Character Does to YOU (And FOR You)

Let's take this up a notch... what happens when you commit to living with character? First, it grounds you. As I've mentioned before, the ability to remain grounded is one of the best traits a person can have. In a noisy, insane world, character is your internal compass. You don't have to please everyone because you know who you are, and you know what matters to you. This kind of grounding brings you peace and stops you from searching for outside approval. You stop second guessing every move and instead, move with intention not with impulse.

Character builds trust not just from others but within yourself. When people see your character in action, they begin to trust you-not just for what you do, but for who you are. People know what to expect from you. You are reliable. There is a quiet dignity in character. People notice how you live. Your reputation carries weight, even in your absence.

People often confuse character with being nice or agreeable. But the true character goes deeper than that. Signs of strong character that don't always get enough credit are the simple things we do, like apologizing when you're wrong, not groveling, but taking ownership. You give people the benefit of doubt; however, you are not naive. You speak up when something's not right, even when it's uncomfortable. And mostly, you stick to your values when no one agrees with you, because character often shows up in the quiet moments, not necessarily in the grand gestures!

So, how do you build character and can you REALLY? Where do you start?

- You must walk the walk and not just talk the talk as I often say. Know the meaning of your core values, not the ones you think you should have, but the ones you actually WANT to live by.

- How do you want to be remembered? This is

a good one because it really makes you think. Once it's all said and done, your reputation is all you have.

- Character starts with being real with yourself. Do you live up to your own standards, and as I said before, do you practice what you preach? Tuning into your own integrity helps your inner alignment.

- Do the right thing, even when it's inconvenient. Whether it's costly, time consuming or eats at your pride, choosing honesty over the simple way out and consistency over impulse is character building.

- Keep your word. As they say, your word is your bond. Whether "I'll call you back" or "I will help you this weekend," small promises build big trust. Every time you follow through on what you say, you'll reinforce that your word means something.

Contrary to that, when you can't keep a commitment, say so, explain why, and own it. It's not about being flawless, it's about being responsible.

- No matter what, surround yourself with people of character. You are who your friends are is the truest statement. If your circle includes people who are thoughtful, trustworthy, and authentic, they'll raise your standard without even trying. Good character is contagious in the best way!

When Character is Challenged

There will be moments in life when living with character doesn't feel so rewarding. For that matter, it might even cost you something. There may be moments when doing the right thing feels incredibly lonely and downright stupid.

But here's the thing: character isn't about who praises you, it's about who you are when you are alone. When you can look yourself in the eye and know you did the best you could with what you had, it brings the kind of peace that doesn't come from applause. It comes from integrity and is worth every hard moment it took.

From the boomerang effect to the ripple effect of character, people may not always remember exactly what you said or did, but they'll remember how they felt in your presence.

They'll remember if you made them feel safe. If you were honest, if you were kind, even when you didn't have to be.

You can inspire people by how you navigate failure. You can also inspire them with how you treat those who can't "do" anything for you. The ripple effect may not be something we can see, but we feel them through the respect we earn, the peace we keep, and the relationships we have nurtured.

Character and Forgiveness

One of the most courageous acts of character is forgiveness.

Holding grudges, staying resentful, or defining people by their worst moments might feel justified, but it erodes your inner peace. Forgiveness is never about pretending nothing happened. It's about refusing to carry the weight of bitterness.

Forgiveness doesn't make you weak; it sets you free.

It's the same as when you forgive yourself. You have created space to grow, heal, and learn.

And finally, character is unquestionably the legacy you leave behind.

There are few things in life we get to control. We don't control our outcome or how others treat us. But we do control this - how we show up to the party!

It's your signature, your quiet power, the legacy you leave behind, long after the meeting ends, the project closes, the conversation wraps up, and the lights go out. We don't boast about character. It's something we embody. Character does the talking for you!

To sum it up, in a world of noise, distraction, and high expectations, character is still one of the quietest, as well as strongest things a person can have!

In order to attain the impossible, one must attempt the absurd.

11

Curiosity and contribution: The Double Whammy!

Some forces in life are powerful on their own. But every now and then, two things come together to create something greater than the sum of their parts like peanut butter and jelly, for example! Here's where curiosity and contribution come in.

On their own, curiosity and contribution are strong ingredients in a well-balanced life. Curiosity keeps you open, learning, expanding. Contribution grounds you in meaning, purpose, and connection to others.

But together? They form a feedback loop of energy, joy, and impact that can transform the way you move through the world.

This chapter isn't about becoming a perfect philanthropist or a walking encyclopedia. It's about approaching life with wonder and purpose-asking questions, finding ways to grow, and using what you've gathered to give something back. It's about being engaged and useful in the truest sense of the words.

Curiosity is one of the first traits we develop as children. We ask "why" 100 times a day. We pull things apart to see how they work. We explore the world with sticky fingers and wide eyes and for a while that wonder carries us through.

Then BAM! Something shifts. We get older! (and SMARTER!) We get busy, and we start thinking we're supposed to have all the answers instead of asking better questions. We stopped being curious. But we all know A CURIOUS MIND IS AN ALIVE MIND!

Curiosity is what keeps us growing. It keeps us humble. It's what allows us to keep being surprised by life in a good way. It means you're open. You're willing to learn.

Curiosity fuels everything from creativity to empathy. It will make you a better listener, keeping your brain flexible and adaptable. It helps you understand people who are different from you as well as make you less judgmental and more compassionate. Curiosity increases your resilience, because you see setbacks as fun puzzles, not dead ends. Curiosity pulls you into possibilities, not paralysis.

So, how does a contribution fit into this you might ask? Contribution is the anchor that grounds you. If curiosity is the spark, contribution is what gives it direction. We all want to feel like we matter, like our life adds up to something more than just running errands and answering emails. Contribution is how we take what we've learned through our curiosity and use it to support or improve the world around us. Contribution doesn't require a charity gala, and, in fact, it is more fun living in the small moments.

Whether it's checking on a struggling friend, sharing your skills with your work comrades, listening with full attention, or helping someone without needing the credit, there are a plethora of ways to contribute without opening your wallet. (Not that that's a bad thing!)

Contribution feeds the soul! When you contribute, you give something meaningful of yourself, allowing you to feel more connected to others. You feel you have a purpose. You also get out of your own head and problems and realize there are things bigger than you. You build confidence through your usefulness and believe it or not, experience a sense of legacy, even in a small way!

Curiosity and contribution are Better Together because when blended, they create vitality! Curiosity fuels your growth where contribution gives that growth a place to land. You turn your insight into impact! Instead of hoarding your knowledge, you share it by creating healing.

It becomes a beautiful cycle when you give. You learn, you grow, you reflect, and you learn some more! When you feel stagnant, look for inspiration. Don't stop learning and use contribution to also refresh your own soul.

That's why balance matters because constant giving or giving too much can lead to burnout. If you're always pouring out without refreshing your own will, your contribution becomes mechanical and eventually resentful. We don't need to be perfect. You can be the mentor who keeps learning! Stay attuned to your emotions and if one side feels dry, you know where to lean next.

Real life double whammies happen in everyday life. That mentor who keeps learning and stays curious and open to change. The parent who asks questions instead of lecturing, and models both engagement and contribution. The friend who asks and acts. They ask, "How are you really?" and then they do something with the answer. Whether they bring soup, send a funny video, or just show up and sit beside you, that's the Double Whammy I am talking about!

When you keep curiosity and contribution alive and balanced, you stay teachable. Your curiosity and collaboration make you a generous human being who doesn't hoard information or look down on others for lack of knowledge. If you are ready to cultivate a Double Whammy approach to life, start with these small tips.

- Start by Noticing What Lights You Up:

Curiosity often lives in what delights you, intrigues you, or even irritates you in a meaningful way! Pay attention to those moments as they are your best clues.

- Ask Better Questions:

Instead of: Why is this happening to me?

Try: “What can I learn from this?"

Instead of: “How Can I fix them?”

Try: "How can I show up well in this situation?"

Better questions unlock deeper growth and in turn, healthier contribution.

- Practice Micro Contributions: You don't need a platform. You just need presence. Say the kind thing. Offer your help. Share your own story. Contribute to the mood of a room, and most of all, give people dignity. That's all part of contribution.

- Connect the Dots:

If you've been learning something or reflecting deeply, ask yourself, "How can I use this to help someone else?"

And if you've been giving a lot, ask, "When is the last time I gave myself space to explore, learn, or question?"

The end result of curiosity, contributing, and staying completely alive, is when you combine these first two. Life doesn't just pass you by. It becomes something you're ENGAGED WITH, from both the inside and outside.

In Summation:

You stay open because you're always learning.

You stay grounded because you're always giving.

You stay connected because your growth and your generosity are in total sync.

It's a beautiful way to live – don't dismiss it or be in a rush to prove yourself but maintain a rhythm of wonder and usefulness which makes you feel happy and alive every day.

Asking, learning, and growing, helps you offer, help, and lift.

So, go ahead! Embrace the Double Whammy. Be curious. Be generous. Let life teach you... and watch your life touch others in a remarkable way!

Because we don't need to have all the answers. We just need to stay engaged with the questions and willing to pass on what we've learned all along the way!

The more you celebrate your life, the more there is in life to celebrate.

12

Celebration

YOU DID IT!!! You made it through the messes, the changes, the challenges, and the quiet victories that no one else saw but you. You showed up again and again. You chose growth when it would have been easier to shut down. You practiced compassion, confidence, curiosity, contribution, and so many other beautiful, hard earned "C" words.

And now, we've finally landed at one of the most powerful words of all: CELEBRATION!

Because what's the point of doing all this work-learning, evolving, balancing, and setting boundaries, if you're not going to enjoy your life?

Seriously, what's the point?

Celebration is more than parties and confetti. It's a MINDSET. It's a decision to notice what's good and right in the world. To take joy seriously. To protect your inner peace. To allow yourself to feel proud, even when no one is clapping. To laugh as much as you can, rest when you need it, and dance like no one is watching.

So, let's talk about what it means to live a life that you CELEBRATE!

Celebrating life as it is (not as you wish it were) is what I am referring to. All the narratives say we should wait to celebrate until something big happens whether it be a promotion, engagement, weight loss, new house, or anything else that makes you want to pop champagne. Those things make you feel worthy of joy. But forget that. Let's flip it to celebrate first! Celebrate for no reason at all!

You're not waiting for some milestones to feel alive. You already are. You're not postponing happiness until everything is perfect... because my guess is, that will never come – just saying. You're choosing joy, even while things are unfinished, imperfect, or still in progress. You, my friend, are the reason to celebrate!

Life is full of settled magic – ordinary miracles that happen every single day.

If you don't learn to notice those things, you'll miss 95% of the good stuff. What a waste! You have a chance to celebrate! Celebration shouldn't be an afterthought and instead, should be a DAILY PRACTICE. Wake up in the morning to remind yourself why today is going to be your

BEST DAY EVAAH!!

Don't let the "Nay Sayers" put a cramp in your style. Let them look at you with envy and awe.

Joy is not frivolous. Let's get one thing clear - joy is not a luxury nor an extra in a movie. It's not a bonus that you earn after you've fixed all your flaws or solved the world's problems.

Joy is a necessity. For your health. For your spirit. For your sanity.

It brings color into your life. It restores perspective, even when things get heavy. It gives you incredible strength to keep going.

We are not meant to live in a constant state of seriousness; life is serious enough already. Humans need light and laughter, which creates softness in moments where you feel free and full in the best way. You don't need to apologize for your joy. And never downplay it! Don't think it has to be earned or justified. Joy is not like respect that must be earned.

Celebrating yourself without shame can be tough, especially if you were raised to be humble or even self-critical. But take this to the grave, you are allowed to be proud of yourself and don't forget it!

While we're allowed to say that you have come a long way, you are doing better than you used to, that you handled that situation well, and that you like, and not just like, REALLY like, who you have become. Don't confuse it with arrogance. It's healthy self-respect.

If you don't learn to celebrate yourself, you'll start looking for others to do it for you, and that puts your joy in someone else's hands.

One of the most beautiful things about healthy celebrations is that they don't create comparison. You can celebrate others without shrinking yourself. When you've learned to celebrate yourself, you don't feel threatened by other people's light; you feel energized by it. Not because you're trying to be polite, but because you mean it, which is the best feeling of all. This brings us back to the boomerang effect of kindness and giving. The more you give, the more you receive.

When opening yourself up to a life of joy, the number one thing to remember is not to let toxicity steal your confetti. Celebration needs protection. Let's face it, there will always be people, places, and situations that will try to steal your joy and dim your light. They try to keep you in a cycle of stress or drama. So, guard your joy like it's your job! Like it is sacred. Because it is!

So, celebrate the people in your life. Tell them what you admire about them. Show up, even verbally, when good things happen in their life. Be loud about it and be their biggest fan.

My final words to those that have soaked up every word and have chosen to live their best life starting today are DON'T WAIT!

Whatever you're waiting for, whatever you're telling yourself must happen before you can feel joy, forget about it!

You already have enough reasons.

So, take a breath. Look around.

Notice what's around you. The people. The scenery. What you must be thankful for.

So, raise your glass of water, wine, coffee, it doesn't matter, and say out loud, "This is my life. I've earned it. And I celebrate every messy, convoluted, crazy, exciting, and magical bit of it!"

HERE'S to YOU! To All the "C" Words You've Embraced! To the one You Already Were but Chose to Take Up a Notch. To the One You've Become, as well as to the one who is Still BECOMING.

Now GO FOR IT! Let your joy be big and your life be LOUD with celebration!

Let us be grateful to the people who make us happy; they are the charming gardeners who make our souls blossom.

Gratitude

With Gratitude and Joy!

As this book comes to a close, I want to take a moment, not just to reflect, but to truly honor the people who have helped shape the journey that brought me here. Because the truth is, we don't grow in isolation. The love we receive, the encouragement we're given, the wisdom we absorb, and the strength surrounding us molds us, even if we don't always realize it at the moment.

First and always, I thank my wonderful, beautiful parents, Bernie, and Sel Leed. Though they are no longer here in body, they are with me in every word of this book. Their spirit, their strength, their love, and their unwavering belief in me echo through these pages. I feel them looking down at me from heaven-smiling, cheering, and nodding as if to say, "That's our girl."

You gave me the roots to grow and the wings to fly. You taught me how to live with heart, humor, grit, and grace. I am who I am because of you.

To the friends who have stood beside me-whether in seasons of sunshine or moments when I needed reminding of my own light - thank you; your love has been a mirror, a safety net, and a launching pad. For those who have helped me live the very 'C' words this book is built upon. To every person who ever shared a kind word, sparked a new idea, challenged me to grow, or gave me space to heal, this book holds your fingerprint. Even if we haven't spoken in years, even if you never knew your impact, thank you.

And finally, to you-the reader – thank you for taking this journey with me. Thank you for believing in your own capacity to change, to grow, to love, to reset, and to celebrate.

If this book reminded you of your strength, your softness, your sparkle, or your ability to show up in this world with a little more compassion, coverage, or common sense-then we've done something beautiful together.

Let this not be the end, but the beginning of the life you truly want to live. One filled with joy. With Connection. With Courage. With character. And yes-with Celebration!

With love and gratitude,

Paula B. Leed

About the Author

A nationally reknowned jeweler and designer extraordinaire, Paula Leed spends her joyous time between Rye Beach, New Hampshire, and Palm Beach, Florida. Walking the walk, not just talking the talk, Paula devotes her personal time to volunteering for many causes, not limited to her constant attention to helping those less fortunate.

Nurturing her friendships is a top priority for her, as detailed in her writing. A successful business owner, Paula enjoys every day with her husband, Richard, and her miniature dachshund, Pretzel. This is her fifth book.

Made in the USA
Coppell, TX
30 June 2026

83550498R10079